Contents

The castles and the people

THE CASTLE, A FOCUS OF LIFE IN THE COUNTRYSIDE

The medieval castle was the center of local life, a refuge, a stronghold, a prison, and a home. Here, in times of war, townspeople and countryfolk took refuge behind its walls. Here, in peaceful times, the lord governed his territory, providing work for the peasants and settling their legal disputes. Some castle owners, who abused their power, were able to escape punishment for their misdeeds by withdrawing behind their castle walls. Sometimes the peasants or townspeople rebelled against their lords—in 1381 Wat Tyler led the Peasants' Revolt, and his followers marched in force on London, where the nobles hid in the Tower of London. Very often, though, peasants and lords gave each other mutual support. As late as the 18th century, when the French town of Châteaudun was destroyed by fire, the local people took refuge in the castle, just as they would have done in the Middle Ages, and were sheltered there until their own houses could be rebuilt.

Visit any country in Europe and you will come across castles, some in ruins, some still complete, a good many in the process of being rebuilt by teams of young people. The countries that boast the most castles are Britain, France, Spain, and Switzerland. In France there are about 600—once there were over 6,000! Some of them have been completely restored, like Pierrefonds to the north of Paris; some consist of only a few stones. In Britain some castles are still in use, like Windsor, one of the queen's homes, and Dover, which is still manned by a garrison. In Spain there are no less than 2,000 old castles to be seen, 250 in good condition.

All these castles look different, for every country developed its own style of building. Their style varies, too, according to whether they were built for a king, prince, or nobleman, or whether they were put together quickly and cheaply for a small country baron. They vary, also, according to the kind of landscape they occupy—like Tarasp and Sion, built in the mountains of Switzerland; Caernarvon, which lies beside the sea in Wales; Marienburg, on the banks of a Polish river; or Salses, in the flat countryside of Roussillon, France. The climate makes a difference, too: Coucy, built in the temperate climate of France, was quite different from the massive Krak des Chevaliers, in the stony Syrian desert.

Wherever they stand they are an impressive sight, these castles, with their towering strength. We should remember, though, that although they may look romantic and picturesque, they were built for very practical purposes in times that were tough and warlike.

Silver Burdett Picture Histories

Castles of the Middle Ages

Philippe Brochard
Illustrated by Patrice Pellerin

Translated by Anthea Ridett
from La Vie privée des Hommes: A l'abri des châteaux du Moyen Age
first published in France in 1980 by
Librairie Hachette, Paris

© Librairie Hachette, 1980. Adapted and published in the
United States by Silver Burdett Company, Morristown, N.J. 1985 Printing.

ISBN 0-382-06927-7
Library of Congress Catalog Card No. 80-51439

THE CASTLE BUILDERS

If you've ever spent a holiday by the sea, you'll know what it's like to build a sand castle. It's fun . . . and it's easy. You might think that building a real castle was equally easy, a job anyone could do. But imagine for a moment that you are living in a hostile country, menaced by wild animals and warlike enemies. Imagine you've never seen a picture or photograph of a real castle, that you have no tools for cutting stone, and know nothing about the laws of balance or the weight and strength of different building materials.

Building a castle was in fact a very specialized business. The builders were not trained in a college but learned their skills on the worksite, taught by other builders. In the Middle Ages the word "architect" was not used; they were called "mastermasons." We know something about these men, from the chroniclers who recorded the lives of their patrons, and by studying the contracts drawn up between nobles and their masons. Some mastermasons were only known in a few villages; sometimes a man's name is remembered for a single building, long since vanished. Others are still famous for their work on important buildings, like Master James of St. George, who built a whole chain of castles in Wales for Edward I, and Eudes de Montreuil, master-mason to the French king Louis IX. Often architecture was not their real profession; King Philip the Fair of France employed his tutor Egidio Colonna, who was also a philosopher and theologian.

BUILDING TECHNIQUES

As new and improved building techniques were discovered, the architecture of castles became stronger and more elaborate. In the 10th and 11th centuries the main part of the building, the tower, was made of timber; it was an easy material to work with and could be found in plenty in most European countries. But as smiths smelted more and more iron and forged it into strong, solid tools, stone came increasingly into use. The first stone towers were

THE CASTLE BUILDER'S HANDBOOK

Everyone in charge of building a castle had read or heard of Vegetius, a Roman architect of the 4th century. He wrote a book, *De Re Militare (The Military Institutions of the Romans)*, hoping to restore the power of the Roman Legions. It was copied over and over again and widely read until the 15th century; it directly influenced the design of ramparts and siege engines. But the builders of the 10th to 13th centuries introduced their own innovations as well.

Cross sections of a primitive castle (above) and of a 13th century castle (below).

Richard the Lionhearted

THE KING OF ENGLAND'S FINANCIAL PROBLEMS

In the 12th century the king of England's income was about £12,000 a year. Henry II and his son Richard the Lionhearted often spent a tenth or more of this on castle building. A stone tower or keep cost about £1,000, spread over the 9 years or so it took to build. The keep of Dover Castle, which was exceptionally splendid, cost £3,000.

In 1277 after a rebellion by the Welsh, Edward I started a 25-year castle-building program in Wales. Among these castles Harlech cost £9,500, Conway £14,000 and Caernarvon £27,000. In 1286 a work force of 25,000 men brought in from all over England was working on these three castles.

In all, Edward spent about £80,000 on his Welsh castles, an enormous sum in those days. Sometimes they were left unfinished "for want of money."

square, copying the shape of the timber towers. However, as ever more powerful siege engines were invented, the builders had to make the walls thicker and stronger. Then they realized that curved walls stood up better to undermining and deflected missiles more effectively, so they began to build round towers (called donjons and later, keeps). They began to crown the walls with crenellated battlements and galleries, and machicolations through which stones and boiling liquids could be poured. The walls had round towers set into them pierced with loopholes through which arrows could be shot in every direction, so that there were hundreds of points at which an enemy could be warded off or attacked.

It could take from six months to fifty years to build a castle, depending on how rich the lord was. Of course, it took less time when the building materials could be found on the spot instead of being brought from a distance. The French châteaux of the Île-de-France and the Loire are recognizable by their white walls built of the local limestone. In addition, to ensure that his creation was as strong as possible, the builder in charge made full use of any natural features of the site, choosing a piece of land nearly surrounded by water, or a cliff top or rocky eminence that would provide ready-made defenses which needed only reinforcing. In flat country a castle needed the extra protection of a moat.

Sometimes the builders made use of ancient fortifications, even ruined ones. From their viewpoint, a ruined castle was a half-built castle. Dover, one of the oldest English castles, incorporates the remains of a Roman lighthouse. And one French lord, Henri de Bourbourg, made very ingenious use of a ruined fort. In 1139 he rebelled against his overlord, Arnoul de Guines. In the neighboring countryside lay the site of an old, ruined fortress. Henri sent men secretly to take its measurements, and then had a wooden tower prefabricated in sections. In one night the fortress rose again. Henri retreated inside it, and there was a long siege before Arnoul de Guines was able to overcome his rebellious vassal.

Once he had decided to build a castle, the lord had to be ready to pay for labor and materials.

SYMBOLS OF POWER

To get the best work done, the master-mason employed professionals. On the largest sites you could see several hundred construction workers—masons, carpenters, and laborers of all kinds. They all had to be paid, fed, and sometimes even clothed. The lord of the manor sometimes tried to reduce his costs by making use of unpaid peasant labor; under this system, instead of paying rent or taxes, the local people gave their lord so many days work in return for land, justice, and protection. But there was a limit to the amount of free labor available. The system might allow for ditch-clearing or transporting timber, for example, but often no more than that.

In addition, the lord's ambitions were limited by the amount of money he had. Many castles were never completed; the work stopped halfway through for lack of funds. The more ambitious lords didn't mind getting into debt; some of them ruined themselves in order to get their castles finished. They would borrow from merchants, committing themselves to repayments over a period of several years. If they had an income from tolls collected at a bridge or taxes from a market town, they would hand this over to the moneylender for ten years or more.

In theory a castle was built for reasons of defense, but the lord knew well that once behind its fortified walls he would be in a very powerful position. Every lord was vassal to another, to whom he owed loyalty—but if he disobeyed his overlord he could take refuge in his castle. That was worth getting ruined for! A great castle was the visible symbol of a powerful lord.

THE INHABITANTS

If we went inside a medieval castle, whom would we find there?

The lord lived there, a nobleman or baron, surrounded by his family—his wife and children, sometimes his mother, his unmarried brothers and sisters, and even more distant relatives.

They had a throng of servants to look after them, to prepare their meals, take care of their clothes and jewelry, maintain the armory, conduct religious services (many castles contained a chapel), and look

HACHETTE

MILITARY MANPOWER

By modern standards medieval armies were small. William I conquered England with an army of barely 12,000, and in 1214 the Holy Roman Emperor tried to invade France with only 9,000 men (1,500 horsemen and 7,500 foot soldiers).

At the siege of Calais in 1346 Henry V of England assembled the mightiest army ever seen—32,000 men. And in 1449 the French town of Fougères stood up to an attack by the duke of Brittany with 150 men defending the castle, 250 the town, and 300 in reserve!

THE PARTS OF A CASTLE

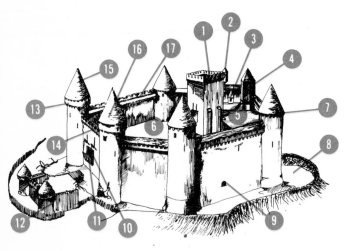

1. Keep	10. Portcullis
2. Watchtower	11. Drawbridge
3. Chapel	12. Barbican
4. Turret	13. Machicolations
5. Inner bailey	14. Crenellations
6. Outer bailey	15. Corner tower
7. Wooden gallery	16. Flanking tower
8. Moat	17. Sentry walk
9. Postern	

after the animals. These people usually came from the neighboring countryside, and the richer the lord the more people would be working in his castle.

The castle was also a fortress, so it would contain a garrison—not, in fact, a very large force. People are always surprised when they come to estimate the military manpower of the Middle Ages. The figures are very low, particularly in comparison with modern armies.

The castle lord could call upon his peasants to fight as part of their duties to him, but the results were not always very satisfactory. Some kings preferred to surround themselves with a defense force of professional soldiers whose only function was to fight. In the 14th century armies were almost exclusively made up of mercenaries, who would be strangers to the region. This presented the lords with a new financial burden—these soldiers would fight only so long as they were regularly paid. The castle owners had to take this into account, and would restrict their garrison to a handful of men, a few dozen or, for the biggest castles, a few hundred. This is why a great deal of attention was paid to the strength of the buildings themselves.

A hidden treasury of pictures

The period called the Middle Ages is still not very well known, yet from that age has survived a treasury of pictures, most of them still waiting to be discovered.

Between the fall of the Roman Empire in the 5th century and the discovery of America in the 15th not only were quantities of castles and cathedrals built, but there were also many artists at work, carving and painting. Their sculptures and murals can be seen in churches and museums, but what are hardly ever seen are the illuminated manuscripts of the times, most of which are hidden away in libraries.

The word manuscript *comes from the Latin and means "written by hand," for of course printing had not yet been invented. These books were copied out on vellum and then "illuminated" in gold or silver and brilliant colors with decorated borders and capital letters, and*

illustrations. The illustrations were called miniatures— not because they were small, but from the Latin word miniare—*to paint or write. Many of these works were "Books of Hours," private prayer books produced for the wealthy. Some contain up to four or five thousand miniatures.*

Occasionally some miniatures are reproduced in magazines or art books, but only a few have been made available to the public by modern printing techniques. So they remain, a truly hidden treasure, waiting to be discovered in libraries and museums.

You can see some of them in the following pages, for each section is illustrated by a miniature, each one telling a story. They show people at work and play, seen through the eyes of medieval artists.

Régine Pernoud

Villages, towns, and castles have been ravaged by war. These people have collected what belongings they could and loaded them onto carts—but where can they go now?

Why castles were built

When a country was at war, towns would be razed to the ground, the countryside pillaged, and fortresses destroyed. The people had to flee wherever they could, defenseless against brigands, wild beasts, and bands of roving marauders. With no castle left to offer them refuge, their chances of survival would be small.

Nowadays the map of Europe is dotted with the remains of castles. What made their builders decide to choose one particular site rather than another?

In the early centuries of the Middle Ages, few countries had a strong central government, some none at all. To protect themselves against invaders like the Vikings, the Arabs, and the Magyars, people built the first fortresses of stone and wood. Later, in the 12th and 13th centuries, vast areas of land were in the hands of a few great noblemen; they had to establish their position and defend their borders— known in those days as "marches." These included the Welsh Marches between England and Wales, the borders between the duchy of Normandy and the lands of the king of France, and those between Christian and Moslem Spain. Meanwhile there had been a big development in trade, and international highways were increasingly important. There were great roads across Europe, some following the course of rivers like the Rhine and Danube, some passing through mountains and along coasts. They all had to be maintained, paid for, and protected by strategically placed castles.

Around the castles peasants worked the land, agricultural settlements developed and villages were built. Protected by the castles, towns sometime grew up; you can tell their origin from their names— Newcastle in England, Castelnuovo in Italy, Neuchâtel in Switzerland, and Châteauneuf and Castelnau in France.

If possible the builder would choose a site with ready-made natural defenses, like a rocky height or a hill. If he had to build on a plain he would have to dig ditches and build extra walls, for the castle had to be strong enough to defend itself and the people who lived around it.

The first castles, like those built by William the Conqueror in England, consisted of a wooden tower on top of a motte (an earthen mound), enclosed by a wooden stockade and, often, a ditch. At the foot of the motte an outer yard called a bailey was also surrounded by a stockade and ditch. These were called "motte and bailey" castles.

roughout history, people under threat of war have sought refuge in rongholds. In Sweden the Vikings surrounded the city of Birka with wall fortified by towers. In the center they made the most of a tural outcrop of rock by building their fortress on it.

After the Roman Empire had fallen to the barbarians, the ordinary folk were left without protection. The inhabitants of towns and villages used the materials of the ancient buildings, taking stones from Roman baths, theaters, and triumphal arches to build fortifications.

fter the Normans conquered England they put up castles every-here to protect themselves against attack, using the English as rced labor. They built wooden towers at first and then stone ones, erched on top of mottes; these were the origin of the castle keep.

mountainous regions, builders could exploit natural features by gging out caves or enlarging existing ones. The resulting fortress as a veritable cave-city. Sites like this can still be seen in vitzerland, Germany, and the Massif Central in France.

Mottes sometimes measured 30 meters across and 12 or 15 meters high; they were encircled by a ditch 4 meters wide and 3 meters deep. It took 100 men 20 days to build one. William the Conqueror appointed barons to live in the castles and rule over the regions.

In the lands of the Holy Roman Empire, power was often held by the Church, which did not hesitate to defend its holdings. In the Pyrenees, and along the Mediterranean where surprise attacks by Arabs were feared, even some churches were fortified.

The skill of the carpenter

The early fortified castles were made of timber. It was a practical building material, quick to use, readily available, and it didn't need mortar to hold it together. A thousand years later the colonists of the Far West and European soldiers in India and Indochina built most of their forts in wood, just like their ancestors in the Middle Ages.

From the 12th century onward, after four or five centuries of intensive clearing, wood became much more scarce. To build one small, simple house required a dozen hundred-year-old oaks. It took 8,000 trees to build the fortress of Trelleborg in Sweden—800,000 square meters of forest!

Even after building in stone had got under way, wood was still needed for defense purposes—for the "hourds," the galleries around the tops of towers, for stockades, and for gates. The art of carpentry also developed when the lords began to want vast meeting halls with timber roofs. As in churches, the techniques used here had originally been perfected by ships' carpenters for constructing the hulls of boats.

Wood was also used to make tools, building equipment, and engines of war. This is where the engineer came in—the word *engineer* originally meant someone who was able to construct and fire siege engines. He was both a carpenter and an artilleryman.

At the same time, the use of wood did not require a highly specialized work force. Most peasants were used to woodcutting or carpentry, so they were a source of useful labor when a castle was being built.

Carpenters at work. The one on the left is cutting a mortise; in the center another is drilling holes with an auger; while the third, on the right, is smoothing a beam with an adze.

...ook two men two hours to cut down a tree measuring a meter
...oss. They would choose a tree that was not too old; if it was over
...0 years old the wood might be rotten. To get the best quality wood
...e woodcutters worked in winter.

...e trunks of oaks were soaked in water through the winter to harden
...e wood. After that they were dried, cut up, and then smoked and
...ted to help preserve them. Seven hundred years later, wooden
...ams that were treated like this are still solid and strong.

...ery part of the castle had to be roofed over—the living quarters,
...stions, and towers. These roofs were tiled with slate, clay, or wood,
...pending on local materials and what money was available. The tiler
...own here wears knee pads to make his work more comfortable.

From the 13th century onwards carpentry became a really skilled
craft. The walls of rooms were lined with decorative wooden panels.
A French architect, Villard de Honnecourt, left a sketchbook of his
drawings, among them the hydraulic saw in the diagram.

Iron tools were expensive. The tools used by medieval carpenters and
joiners were not very different from those used today, as you can see
here. Examples of medieval tools can be seen in museums such as
the Maison de l'Outil at Troyes in France.

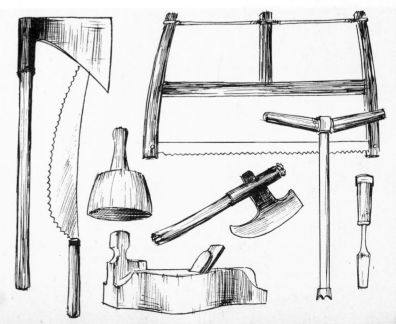

A castle nearing completion. The masons are carrying hods full of mortar over their shoulders.

The building site

The men you can see in this picture, hard at work building a castle, would have lived in the nearest town—unless they were journeymen, who traveled round the countryside offering their services at any building site they came across. Journeymen were professionals, free men who were paid by the day *(la journée)*. Unpaid peasants might lend a hand as part of their service to the lord, but building in stone needed trained men who knew what they were doing. If the job had to be done quickly, a team of laborers would be called in to help them. Beaumaris Castle in Wales, the last of Edward I's castles, was a "rush job"; in the summer of 1295, about 3,500 men were working on it. If the lord ran out of money the masons would not have to go far to find a cathedral, church, or town under construction where their services could be used.

Although the Romans had created a great tradition of stone building, most of the primitive fortresses built between the 6th and 10th centuries were made of timber. Then stone came back into use small stones at first, then progressively larger ones—quarry stones that could be properly shaped. Castles began to have smooth walls, making it difficult for the enemy to find a foothold during an attack. In the 15th century brick began to be used a good deal; it was less expensive and stood up better to artillery fire. Often materials had to be restricted to those that could be found on the spot or close to the site; a team of oxen could draw a load of one and a half tons no further than 9 or 10 miles in a day.

14

dieval walls might be built up to 3 or 4 or even 5 meters thick. They e made of two outer, parallel walls of cut stones, called an ashlar ng, filled in with rubble, cement, and rubbish. Pieces of wood or were inserted to help hold them together.

sons would use a ''squirrel-cage'' windlass and a pulley to raise stones to the top of a wall. With the one shown here a man could ten times his own weight in stones. For lesser heights, the rers would push a loaded barrow up a ramp.

Toward the end of the Middle Ages stone dressing (cutting) became an increasingly complex art. The stonecutter would chisel his personal mark on his work. This indicated who did the job, and helped when the wages were worked out.

The ''architect''—the master-mason—overseeing the work. He was responsible for every stage of the building, from design to completion. He knew all its secrets and later often found himself in charge of its defense. He might also lead an attack against another castle.

development of iron tools enabled stonemasons to cut stones in er blocks with smooth edges and sides, to construct walls which enemy could not mine under or climb up. Other essential pieces of ipment were the mason's set-square and plumbline.

On top of a bare hill, a castle rises, its keep protected by the outer wall and its towers.

The castle's defenses

From the outside the medieval castle looked as austere as a military camp. Let's take ourselves back 700 years, and visit a 13th-century castle.

First of all, you might be surprised at how bare the hillside is. It is kept deliberately cleared of trees and shrubs so that there is nothing to conceal an approaching enemy. Here, too, are the "lists," the enclosures where tournaments and jousting take place. Once we've climbed the hill, we go through the palisade (a wooden stockade) which is the castle's first line of defense. Probably the lord has an orchard growing nearby. Then comes a deep, steep-sided ditch; if it is filled with water it is called a moat.

The surrounding wall, called a curtain wall, is reinforced by wall-towers, also part of the defense system. Along the battlements are machicolations, projecting galleries with holes in the floor through which an attacker can be seen and the defenders can throw stones, boiling liquid, or burning matter on him.

Once through the main gate we find ourselves in the courtyard, called a bailey or ward. This is often divided into two—an inner and an outer bailey. Farther in, towering above the rest and encircled by another curtain wall, stands the keep. The entrance is on the second floor, which is reached by a wooden stairway that can be destroyed if an enemy gets that far. Inside the keep is one large room with a hole in the ceiling through which the upper floors can be reached. This, too, has a destructible ladder, a last resort. There are two floors below ground level where you will find the well, the storerooms, and a trench into which all the castle rubbish is thrown.

was impossible to build a castle on a rocky cliff or a hill, it would be rounded by ditches and a water-filled moat. The water was usually gnant and the moat would have to be cleaned out from time to e—not a pleasant or easy job.

Once the drawbridge had been raised, no one could get into the castle unless they could cross the moat and get past the portcullis and through the gate. The outer end of the bridge was often protected by a small fortified gatehouse called a barbican.

m this viewpoint you can see the inner bailey surrounded by its tain wall. As the centuries went by the lords began to build mselves living quarters here which were much more comfortable homelike than the keep, which was built for military purposes.

A sentry on guard duty. If the castle were attacked the members of the garrison could run quickly to their posts along the sentry walk. Standing on watch for hours could be a cold business; there were small watch towers where the sentries could keep a bit warmer.

outer bailey of the castle was usually buzzing with activity. Here ld be found everything the castle dwellers needed, the most ortant being a well. No community can live without water. The ey was always thronged with servants, peasants, children and

animals. People met here to exchange news and gossip, and farm produce was brought in on carts. There were craftsmen's workshops, too, for the potter, saddler, joiner, and blacksmith. Beneath the castle walls, in fact, was a miniature city.

A clerk teaches the lord's children in the library.

Inside the lord's private residence

Now let's take a look inside the lord's home. In the 12th century we would find one huge room containing little more than a fireplace, a bed, and a chest or two. The only other items of furniture were the trestles on which planks were laid to make a table when it was needed (hence the expression "laying the table").

Two centuries later we would find the lord's residence completely transformed. The living area was now divided into small rooms, better decorated, with more privacy and, above all, warmer. People no longer slept in the same room where they ate. There were cupboards where they could keep their personal possessions and tableware, and fine furniture was a status symbol. Behind the bedchamber was a "wardrobe," a room where clothes were stored, with washing and toilet arrangements attached.

The lord also set aside some space for his library. There a clerk (a member of the clergy) could use the books to educate the lord's children. The miniature above shows us a reading desk, bookshelves, and a revolving bookcase. All the books are protected by thick leather covers and metal clasps. The pupils are seated on a kind of mattress; only the teacher has a proper chair. At this period wealthy people began to hang tapestries and carpets on their walls, which added warmth and intimacy to the rooms.

lords wanted to be able to move quickly in case of war. So in the y castles, furniture was scanty. Chests doubled as seats and there e no real tables. At mealtimes, servants laid planks on top of tles, and people sat on benches.

The huge living rooms were cold and drafty. Here the lady of the castle is having tapestries hung to divide one big room into smaller, warmer units. Tapestries also provided colorful forms of decoration, as did the wall paintings which enlivened the walls of the finest castles.

e early Middle Ages the lord and lady slept in a room adjoining the t hall of the keep. By the 13th century, however, they had :hambers which were private and more comfortable. At night, ry curtains were drawn around the bed to keep in the warmth.

In the early days, the great hall was the heart of the castle. Everyone lived and slept here. But when castle rooms became smaller in the 13th century, the hall was chiefly used as a meeting room for the lord and his vassals.

r the evening meal the lord of the castle liked to join his wife and dren before the fireside, to listen to a minstrel singing songs or ing tales of noble deeds. It was the hour for storytelling, and for ›anging gossip and jokes. In the 15th century there was more

furniture. Eating and drinking vessels made of silver or pewter were kept in special chests. The vessels were very valuable, so the chests were kept locked.

The scribe writes down the lord's orders. After the lord has affixed his seal, they are entrusted to a messenger.

The lord and his household

Life revolved around the lord. It was he who decided to build or enlarge the castle, he who organized its defense and directed the fighting in the event of an attack. He had to see that his lands were properly cultivated, and from time to time introduce improvements in farming life. He upheld the religious life of the community, making gifts and payments to the clergy. His most important decisions were recorded on parchment and sealed with his personal mark. He ruled as master, but in turn he had to answer for his acts to his overlord—the king or a very important nobleman who had granted him his lands.

In order to fulfill all these obligations, he employed a number of servants who had specific duties; they included a chamberlain, a treasurer, a steward, a butler, and often many others.

In private, the lord took great care of himself, and his morning toilet was an important event. If it

was the fashion, he might wear a beard or moustache but more often he was clean-shaven, like the noble man shown here. His hair was carefully combed and even perfumed. He dressed with care, putting on clothes of the best materials—a shirt of fine Flemish linen, a robe of Italian velvet trimmed with furs from Scandinavia, and shoes of Italian or Spanish leather.

Until the 10th century, nobles were not usually well educated; very few knew how to read or write. But then culture began to spread. Some members of the nobility, especially in France, composed poetry and music or wrote histories of their family or region. One of these was William the Troubadour, Duke of Aquitaine. Lords entertained local artists or invited them to come from elsewhere. A French poet, Guiot of Provins, left descriptions of no less than eighty-six castles whose lords made him welcome.

castle was the center of a self-supporting community. Under the dal system the castle protected the surrounding countryside, and return the peasants owed the lord certain duties. They also had a ht to use the land and live off its produce. After the harvest, at Michaelmas (at the end of September) or the feast of Saint Remy (in early October) they brought the lord a certain proportion of the food they produced. These peasant families worked the same strips of land for centuries, in return for the same dues.

assal places his hands between those of his overlord; by this act of omage" he promises to be the lord's man (*homme* in French) and ears obedience to him. In return the lord undertakes to protect him d grants him a piece of land, which is then known as his "fief."

ry lord was master of his lands, provided he respected the local toms. If he didn't, his overlord would call him to order. He ntained law and order, and dispensed justice, deciding legal butes between his peasants.

In the late Middle Ages noblemen were very conscious of their appearance and personal hygiene. They liked their clothes to be taken good care of. Every morning they washed thoroughly and they often took a hot, scented bath. Sometimes their wives would join them.

The chancellor puts the lord's seal on a document dictated by his master. Signatures didn't come into use until the 15th century, but seals have existed for 5,000 years; they were often engraved on signet rings. When a man died his seal would be destroyed or buried.

A lord visits his lady to pay her homage before he sets off for war.

The lady of the castle

From the start, a girl would be involved in the life of the castle. As a child she would run freely in the courtyards and living rooms, playing games of soldiers with her brothers and sleeping in her parents' room. When a visitor arrived it was her role to do him honor by serving his meal and making him comfortable.

But once the boys began training to be knights, she had to acquire the traditional feminine arts. She had to learn to dress and wear jewelry attractively, and do her hair elaborately. She spent her time drawing or tapestry making.

When she grew up she had a right to privacy; no one entered her room without showing proper respect, particularly if she was wearing an indoor gown, like the lady in the miniature shown here. As you can see, the men-at-arms in the doorway are hesitating, awed by the delicate floor tiles, the carpet,

hangings, and cushions.

Ladies liked to spend their time listening to the songs of minstrels, but they also enjoyed hunting and tournaments. When their husbands were away they were in sole charge of the domain, but married women had very few rights and were subordinate to their husbands. They did have some financial independence—on her marriage a lady would be given a piece of land by her father, while her husband also made her a gift of land. If she was widowed she kept this dowry. She was entitled to manage her own property and keep the income from it.

Despite her low status, a woman of character could play quite a strong role—like Adèle de Blois, William the Conqueror's daughter. When she learned that her husband Etienne had given up his crusade, she decided he should pull himself together and made him go back!

In the 13th century the custom of making wax models to represent the Nativity (started by Saint Francis of Assisi) became popular. Here the lady of the castle has brought her children to admire the Holy Family. Until they were 7 she was in charge of their education.

Women and girls specialized in spinning and embroidery, while weaving was mainly a man's job. By the 15th century, cloth was woven mostly in the towns, where the weavers formed themselves into guilds. Their tapestries helped warm the cold castle.

In the Middle Ages everyone loved dressing in bright colors. Traveling merchants would visit the castle, sure of a good welcome, with their silks from the East or brocades from Italy. They were also sure of making a lot of money—unless the king decided to tax luxury goods!

These paupers have not been able to find shelter with a charitable foundation—the neighboring monastery or the "hospital," where the poor were cared for. They wander along the roads, begging for alms. The lady comes to their aid; this is part of her religious duty.

The lord's wife is overseeing the servants, who are strewing rushes and herbs on the floor. This was the usual way of covering the floor, which was often simply bare earth, or chilly flagstones. Only the richest nobles could afford carpets. The floors got very dirty!

The king of France, back from a successful campaign, is welcomed at the city gates.

The royal tours

This miniature shows the king of France being greeted with all due honor by officials of the Church. The artist has taken pains to make the royal figure stand out: he has painted him on a white horse decked out in gold and draped with a cloth decorated with fleur-de-lys—the royal emblem of lilies. The king's armor is all of gold, in contrast to his steel-clad knights and men, and his long cloak is lined with ermine. To show that this is an official visit he wears a crown and carries the scepter, symbol of his royal power. Behind him a knight carries his banner.

To acquire all this power had been a hard-fought battle lasting five centuries. Before the 10th century few European monarchs would have been greeted with such respect; they were "peers," equal to any other lord. During the early Middle Ages they had to fight for their position against ambitious lords

and barons, and against each other. So they traveled through their kingdoms, making their power felt in matters of government and law, and keeping down unruly lords by controlling castles. No one could build a castle without permission from the king, and when a lord was suspected of hatching rebellion the king would nip it in the bud by having his castle pulled down.

Over the centuries royal power became established in England, Spain, and France. In the 12th century the Plantaganet king of England Henry II owned not only England but huge areas of France, and he traveled ceaselessly to keep his lands in order, choosing reliable men to govern in his absence. By the end of the Hundred Years' War in 1453 France had expanded from a relatively small kingdom, and only Calais was left in English hands.

gs had to maintain their authority, but their vassals—the great ls and the barons—wanted to keep their independence. To keep m in order the king would travel through his territory; his journey s called a "royal progress." He would go from castle to castle, where the lords had to receive their guest with all the splendor they could muster. The entire court would travel with the king, including the queen and her ladies, followed by a convoy carrying cooking equipment, food, clothing, and sometimes even the crown jewels.

ns were minted by hand, so they were not perfectly shaped, and honest dealers used to clip the edges to take some of the precious tal. People were licensed to mint coins under the king's supervi-; in England the Royal Mint was in the Tower of London.

A lady going through the documents she has dictated to a secretary (a clerk) and sealing them with an oval seal. Only queens and noble-women could exercise the power of government, but some of them ruled whole kingdoms, like Blanche of Castile.

king did not build fortresses just to defend his country against asion: the castle was a symbol of his royal power. Many castles e used as prisons, like the Tower of London (below). Built by liam the Conqueror, it became a prison in the 12th century.

Life at court was fairly simple until the 15th century. Then lords of very rich estates, like the dukes of Burgundy, began to organize their lives with a great deal of pomp and ceremony. It was not long before other lords and kings began to copy them.

Life in the countryside

We know that during the Middle Ages there were some major changes in the climate. Memoirs written at the time, as well as other evidence, tell us that the 12th and 13th centuries were definitely mild, with colder weather in the following centuries. Changes in the weather and the cycle of the seasons had major effects on life both inside the castle and in the countryside around. A too rainy summer meant a small harvest and fewer supplies to store against siege, while horses and men struggled ankle-deep in mud. Too hot a summer, on the other hand, could dry up moats and wells—a disaster for people in a besieged castle. A cold, dry winter increased the risk of fire and attracted hungry wolves and bears, while a rainy winter encouraged the spread of serious diseases. One such disease was the bubonic plague, which spread across Europe from Asia in 1348–1349. This disease, which the Europeans called the Black Death, killed about one fourth of the population of Europe.

Except in the south of France and in Italy, most castles were built in the countryside, and another influence on country life was the lord himself. He could use his wealth to improve conditions for the population by building roads and canals. He could get the king's permission to have a market set up at the foot of his castle walls. He might get on good terms with the local monastery—and earn himself a reputation as a good Christian—by promising to build a chapel or to shelter pilgrims. And he could get more land cleared and cultivated by granting special privileges and encouraging newcomers to settle on his land—particularly after the Black Death when the working population had shrunk and peasants were able to demand more freedom and payment for their work.

July. Peasants peacefully harvesting, and shearing their sheep at the foot of the Château de Poitiers. This illustration is from the *Très Riches Heures du Duc de Berry,* a famous and beautiful Book of Hours.

the first signs of fine weather in March and April, the peasants
gan hoeing and weeding the soil before sowing for the summer
rvest. Plots of land were cultivated within the castle walls to help
ovide food in case of a siege.

The lord and his retinue ride out on a fine spring day. Riding and
hunting continued through the winter, and they must have been glad
of the warmth of spring after all the rain and cold weather. In March
or May the lord would invite his vassals to join his hunting parties.

summer the harvest was reaped, threshed, and gathered in. When
e last cartload of sheaves had been stacked the peasants could
ax for a while and enjoy the harvest celebrations, knowing that the
stle was supplied with food for the next year.

October and November the castle folk spent the last fine days
king their sheep to pasture and sowing next year's crops. Grain
nted in the fall would be harvested the following spring. Farmers
d to take good care of their plows because they were expensive.

Food was stored in the castle cellars, attics, and storerooms. This
work was done by "serfs," peasants who were not allowed to leave
the lord's lands and had to give him a certain number of workdays
every year in exchange for their own strips of land.

In winter the peasants continued the work of cutting hedges
and clearing away the bushes and shrubs around the castle
walls. Hunting was easier now; so was poaching, of course, though
severe punishments awaited poachers who got caught.

Baking bread in the castle of the duke of Burgundy in France

Provisions for the year

The inhabitants of the castle tried to be self sufficient. There was always the possibility of a war, and trade was irregular, with bandits infesting the highways, so they produced as much of their own food as possible. Thus the castle was not just a military fortress; it was the nerve center of a whole region, large or small, which had to keep it supplied with provisions. Within this area was the lord's *demesne*—his own land, including farmland and the woods and heathland where he hunted. Beyond it lay the peasants' cottages and the fields they worked to produce their own food, some of which went to the lord. The estate had to supply everything—food for all, building materials, wool, cloth, and leather. Only items like salt and a few luxuries were imported from elsewhere.

The two main sources of energy were wood and water. Wood was burned wherever fire was needed, from the smith's furnace to the castle ovens and fireplaces. Water power turned the wheels of the

mills that ground grain to make flour, pigments to make dyes, clay for pottery, and even iron ore. Water had the added advantage of being full of fish. Even in the 12th century when people began to build windmills, rivers were still useful. The wind may drop but a river never stops running—unless it ices up in winter. But then in winter, all activities slowed down, and people lived off the provisions they had stored in summer.

Getting the stores in was a major operation in which everyone was involved. The grain had to be harvested, grapes or apples pressed for wine or cider, meat and fish preserved by salting or smoking. Quantities of loaves had to be baked, as we can see in the picture here, which shows the kitchen of the duke of Burgundy's castle. It's easy to understand why lords preferred to be paid in food and labor rather than money!

28

Windmills appeared in western Europe towards the end of the 12th century. Only rich landowners like lords and abbots could afford to build them, or sometimes groups of ordinary people. The mill owner took a fee from people who brought their grain to be ground.

To light the castle at night, people made their own candles. Beeswax or muttonfat was melted over a fire and poured into molds. There were also oil lamps and torches of resinous wood.

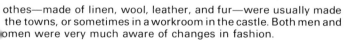

Clothes—made of linen, wool, leather, and fur—were usually made in the towns, or sometimes in a workroom in the castle. Both men and women were very much aware of changes in fashion.

The lord allowed the peasants to use his winepress, like his mill, in return for a fee. It was an enormous machine and very expensive to build, requiring a great deal of wood for its construction.

It was important to use every means of preserving food. Stores were kept underground, where it was cool. In the huge fireplaces fish and meat were dried or smoked. In the castle cellars stood huge stone troughs full of salt for preserving ham and bacon.

A 15th-century banquet. The guests sit at a separate table, and musicians entertain the diners.

A medieval banquet

As the centuries went by, both food and table manners became more refined. Before sitting down at table everyone washed their hands carefully, since they ate with their fingers. The lord or his chaplain said grace, and if guests had been invited to a banquet the meal might go on for hours, with entertainment by musicians and jesters.

During Lent visitors would have to make do with four of five different dishes of fish caught in the local streams or ponds; from the 13th century on, mackerel and herring, salted or smoked, would be delivered from the coast. Salmon was never offered to a guest; that was an everyday food, which the poor ate. A proper banquet included several different meat dishes: beef, pork, chicken, and game, boiled or

roasted, and accompanied by hot or cold sauces, highly spiced. Only a few green vegetables were served, in season. The potato was quite unknown, but people ate a great deal of bread—over a pound a day.

A heavy meal like this would make the diners thirsty. In western Europe the usual drink was cider; in England there was ale, and mead, made from honey; in the north people drank barley beer. Water was pleasant to drink if it came from a spring or well; if it was kept in a cistern people added wine, licorice, or honey to disguise the stale taste. But the favorite drink of the nobility was wine, and if the lord could not produce it on his own land he would have to import it, at great expense.

ate as the 15th century thick slices of bread were used as plates at nary meals. At the end of the meal they would be given to the , or to the lord's hounds. Furniture was sometimes richly orated, like the sideboard you can see here.

In the 12th century people started using two-pronged forks as well as their fingers. Until then the only implement used at table was the point of one's knife. Here a guest is offering the lady some food on the end of his fork, so she can keep her fingers clean.

es of curdled milk were popular. To make "larded milk": (1–2) the milk with sliced bacon fat, saffron, and beaten eggs until the ure curdles. (3) Leave to drain overnight. (4) Cut into thick slices fry. (5) Decorate with cloves or pine nuts, and serve.

Kitchens were often huge, with open fires for roasting and enormous baking ovens. As meals sometimes lasted several hours, the food was kept hot in metal dishes. For cooking, the kitchen workers used clay dishes, made in the castle pottery.

e 15th century cooks tried to please their masters by making s that looked magnificent. Cakes and sweets were decorated in lors of the rainbow, and roast birds—pheasants, peacocks, and s—were dressed up in their feathers so that they looked alive.

A lord plays his favorite game of chess, surrounded by his friends and the castle garrison.

Games and pastimes

This picture tells us quite a lot about the home life of a lord. We can see that it was drawn at a peaceful time, for the knights and soldiers are shown relaxing and chatting indoors; probably the weather was bad that day, for a servant has hung a piece of tapestry over the fireplace to stop the wind blowing down the chimney. The windows have glass in them, a rare luxury, even in the late Middle Ages.

A knight has just brought some urgent news for the lord, interrupting his game of chess. Chess was a popular indoor game with men because the board reminded them of a battlefield on which they maneuvered their pieces like soldiers—and the most important pieces were knights and castles. But in chess, brains were more important than brawn.

If the lord had received a good education he might also spend some spare time reading in his library. His books would include some stories of chivalry, like Sir Thomas Malory's tales of King Arthur, *Le Morte d'Arthur,* and romantic poems like the French *Romance of the Rose.* There were some religious works, too, and most important of all the Bible.

The lord's wife was fond of listening to the tales of minstrels, recited or sung to music. Music was a very important form of entertainment. Some lords composed pieces themselves and wrote poetry; their castles became centers of cultural life.

Castles, however, were built for wartime defense, and in peacetime the days could drag. A famous 12th-century troubadour, Bertrand de Born, once wrote, "I do not love peace." To escape the boredom some lords left home to go on crusades, often taking their wives with them. And some set off on amazing real-life adventures, journeys of exploration to the ends of the world as it was then known—Russia, Asia Minor, and Africa.

The most popular indoor games were checkers, tables (a kind of backgammon popular with ladies), and above all chess. At the end of the 14th century, playing cards made their appearance in Europe from the East. They came in a great variety of designs.

In the Middle Ages music and poetry went together. Instruments included the lute, the hurdy-gurdy, the flute, the rebec (an ancestor of the violin, shown above), the tabor (a long narrow drum), organs which were often portable), the harp, and the guitar.

Grownups enjoyed playing Blind Man's Buff. In England it was called "Hoodman Blind"; the chief player wore a hood over his head. In France it was called "Colin au Maillet" in memory of the knight Colin no, blinded in the siege of Liège in 999, still fought on.

People enjoyed games of skill or chance. They were only supposed to play with dice on fair, or market, days, but they often gambled secretly in taverns. They played for money, sometimes even for clothes or weapons.

On Sundays or holidays the people from the nearest village met the castle folk for a game of quoits or a ball game, like the one below, which was played with curved clubs and a leather ball. It was a rough game, the ancestor of present-day hockey.

Holidays and festivals

Life in the Middle Ages was not easy, but there were plenty of holidays and people knew how to enjoy them!

First there were the lord's family occasions; betrothals, marriages, births, baptisms, and even funerals all provided a good excuse for putting on one's best clothes to feast and dance. Sometimes the lord took his wife and children to join the celebrations of a peasant family; in the 15th century there were complaints about such undignified behavior by people who thought it wrong for the nobility to rub shoulders with their tenants in this way.

All the same, throughout the Middle Ages, the castle and village got together to celebrate the Church festivals. There were over 100 holy days (holidays) a year in honor of Christ or one of His saints, plus the long holidays at Christmas, Easter, and Whitsuntide. Festivals were fewer in summer-

time; between Midsummer Day at the end of June and Michaelmas at the end of September everyone was too busy working in the fields or away making war. But there were plenty of feast days in winter and spring. The Christmas celebrations went on for twelve days, through New Year's Day until Twelfth Night, when a traditional cake was eaten. Sometimes during Christmas the nobility and peasants changed places and the "Lord of Misrule" took charge. Then there was Candlemas, with a candle-lit procession, Shrove Tuesday, Easter, and May Day, when people carried green branches in honor of the spring.

Although most holidays were Christian festivals, the church often kept up traditions that had been handed down from pagan times and were related to sun worship and other cults; these included May Day and Midsummer Day customs.

Lords and ladies dance in the open air on a fine spring day. This is an illustration to the famous poem *The Romance of the Rose.*

On Holy Thursday the lord washed the feet of the poor on his estates. This symbolic gesture was ordered by the Church to remind the rich and powerful that Christ Himself washed the feet of His disciples.

Entertainers—acrobats, animals trainers, jugglers, and dancers—traveled the roads performing at fairs and markets. Sometimes they would entertain the lord and lady, and if the lord was generous he would give them food and lodgings for a day or two.

Although life was hard people had plenty of chances to enjoy themselves—over 100 holidays a year! Many were religious festivals, like Christmas, when the lord, his lady, and all the people in the castle attended Mass in the castle chapel.

A wedding was a good excuse for letting off steam. Everyone joined in, dancing and singing. If there were not enough musical instruments to go round they seized anything they could make a noise with, and they all banged and shouted and sang.

At the end of June, when Midsummer Day arrived, everyone got together for a final fling before the heavy work of the summer started. A bonfire was lit in honor of the longest day, and the young men showed off by leaping over the flames.

Egged on by a huntsman, the excited pack falls on a dying boar.

Hunting—a sport and a necessity

Our picture shows the final moment of a hunt—the kill. The quarry, wounded and exhausted, has given up the struggle. The hounds, at fever pitch after several hours of hunting, fall on the dying boar and tear it to pieces.

One of the lord's chief amusements was hunting. But it was more than just a sport—it was a necessity. From time immemorial men had had to fight wild animals to protect their own lives; in the Middle Ages they still had to kill boars, rabbits, and foxes to protect their crops and chickens. Worse, in some countries people were still attacked by bears, and in Britain and elsewhere wolves still roamed the forests.

Hunting was also an important source of food; venison and game were often eaten. And in addition, hunting was one of the best ways for the lord and his men to keep in training for warfare. The lord would be in the saddle all day long, following the animal's scent, riding across rivers and through ponds, galloping tirelessly across country. At the day's end he would use his dagger to finish off the quarry. (He always rode his warhorse, who was not afraid of wild beasts.)

Man did not hunt alone: he had his allies, the hounds. Every castle had its own pack, made up of several different breeds including scenting hounds; greyhounds, prized for their speed; and wolfhounds, strong enough to bring down a boar or a deer. In some countries hunters even used falcons and cheetahs.

The peasants could not afford the equipment for this kind of hunting. They had to track the smaller animals, often using ferrets, which could squeeze themselves into the burrows. In addition, the privilege of hunting became more and more reserved for the upper classes, who made it a science, and even a kind of art. Eventually the peasants were strictly forbidden under severe penalties to engage in this activity.

arning the skills of hunting was part of a young nobleman's
ucation. The lord put his son in the hands of an experienced
ntsman, who taught him to recognize the tracks of animals. If there
d been a snowfall the prints were much easier to see.

Hunting helped rid the countryside of dangerous animals. In the 12th century, when the count of Zähringen decided to build a stronghold, his men had to kill off the bears on the chosen site. Later, it became the city of Berne in Switzerland, where bears are still kept on show.

uipment for hunting was the same as for fighting—bows and
ows, pikes or lances, and daggers. Hunters also set traps for larger
imals, digging pits and disguising them with leaves, or making
works of rope which would entangle the animal as it ran past.

Hawking was another popular sport, a delicate and graceful art particularly enjoyed by women. Hawks, falcons, and other birds of prey were captured and trained to bring down other birds and small animals. Between flights they were kept on a leash, wearing a hood.

nting was a necessity, but the lords thoroughly enjoyed it, too.
ly noblemen could afford to hunt like this with packs of hounds and
etinue of huntsmen and servants. Part of the pleasure was to stop
d picnic in the open air, with hot dishes prepared by servants in a

traveling kitchen. The hunt would often cover very long distances in pursuit of a stag. Sometimes they would get lost and would have to ask for hospitality in the house of a vassal or in a peasant's hut.

In the lady's bedchamber a nurse and a maidservant tend the newborn baby.

From the cradle to the grave

The birth of a baby was a joyful event in the castle. All the work the lord put into looking after his estates would be wasted if he had no heir to leave them to. A boy baby meant there would be someone to carry on his life's work. If the child was a girl, she would have to be married to a neighboring lord who would look after the estates in the same way. Marriages were often arranged while the children were too young to have any choice in the matter; their feelings were not considered important. Of course, when the estate covered only a few villages, its future was not so important. But when the lord happened to be the king of England or the duke of Aquitaine, his children's marriages were of concern to everyone.

The tiny creature in the cradle would receive the greatest care and attention from his mother, his nurse, and all the servants, for everyone knew how fragile babies were. Until quite recent times the life of a small baby was a precarious thing, and many died in infancy. Until the 14th century the average length of life was longer than it became thereafter. Between 1315 and 1317 there were two years when it never stopped raining and famine ravaged the whole of Europe. This was followed in 1348 by the Black Death, the plague which struck down one person in three and wiped out whole villages. The morale and health of the survivors were deeply affected, and people died earlier. A writer of the period said "The world will never be able to regain its old strength." Even royalty declined. Charles VI of France became mad, and when he died at the age of fifty-three, he had the appearance of extreme age.

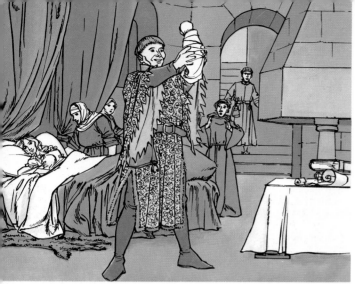

lord's wife has just given birth to a son. Let's imagine they are ng to call him Bertrand. Will he have a future? He could die of any nber of childhood illnesses which we have learned to cure or vent only in the 20th century.

the age of 15 Bertrand becomes a squire, attendant to a knight. At he has his first taste of battle and proves he is a man, able to stand to an adversary. When he has completed his training in the next r or two he will become a knight himself.

Until the age of 7, Bertrand stays close to his mother, but after that he starts his training for knighthood. He is given a basic education by a clerk—a priest or monk—but he prefers his combat training. He wants to be a worthy successor to his father.

Out hunting, young Sir Bertrand meets a beautiful girl and suddenly feels embarrassed by his dirty clothes. He is 22, old enough to marry. But he will be able to marry for love only if his father has not arranged a match for him with the daughter of a neighboring lord.

Sir Bertrand dies at the age of 40, exhausted by ill health and war wounds. His wife will mourn him a long time, for he was a brave knight and a loyal husband. His children will have a tombstone carved in his memory.

The code of chivalry

In the early part of the Middle Ages lords and knights were a rough and ready lot, not noted for gentleness or for showing mercy to their enemies. Gradually, however, the code of chivalry developed—a system of ideal conduct by which knights were supposed to live. It was strongly encouraged by the Church and also by women, who preferred courteous behavior to rough manners. By the 13th century chivalry had become the highest ideal of the medieval knight—even if they didn't all live up to it. All over Europe people were reading romances written in praise of the virtues that are still called "chivalrous." And even today people still write books and make films about the heroes of chivalry, like King Arthur and his Knights of the Round Table.

To become a knight a man had to fulfill certain requirements: he had to keep his word, defend the weak, show generosity to all—in fact he had to respect an entire code of honor. The code was never written down, but everyone was aware of it.

Christianity was an important element of chivalry. A knight had to uphold the faith and the teachings of the Church, attend Mass, and fast on Fridays, and ultimately fight against the Infidel. His personal life had to be equally high-minded; his sword must be used to defend the weak, the orphan, and the poor, and to punish evil-doers. He had moral obligations, too: to show mercy to a disarmed enemy, to come to the help of a companion in trouble, and above all to be loyal to his lord.

Nobles did not automatically become knights. Lords—even kings—had to earn their knighthood and go through a ceremony of "dubbing." But in the 14th century some nobles started creating knights by the dozen, and the idea of chivalry began to deteriorate.

This picture of a knight in full armor was painted around 1450.

e young squire was made a knight in the springtime, when he was
out 18. He spent the whole of the previous night praying in the
apel. In the morning he took communion and his sword was
essed. He was expected to use it only in an honorable cause.

The squire was "dubbed" a knight by an older knight, who gave him
the "accolade" by striking him on the shoulder with his hand or
sword. The new knight then leaped onto his horse, fully armed, to
show off his ability as a horseman and warrior.

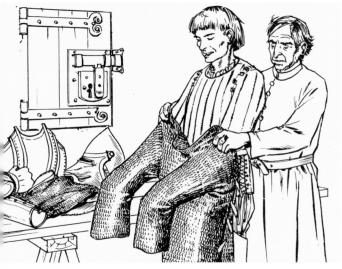

was quite complicated getting into one's armor, and knights had to
helped. First came the aketon, a kind of padded tunic; and over that
ongsleeved shirt of mail, the hauberk. In the 14th century plates of
eel were added, which later evolved into the suit of armor.

If a knight rebelled against his overlord or committed some crime, he
was severely punished. He was "degraded" by the removal of his
sword and spurs and banished from his lord's lands. From then on he
was a lonely figure, wandering the roads, trusted by no one.

encourage loyalty and knightly virtues, several lords and princes
unded orders of knights. These included the Order of the Knights
mplar and the Knights of St. John, who defended Christianity in the
ly Land. Edward III of England, who admired the tales of King

Arthur, founded the Order of the Garter; King John of France founded
the Order of the Star; and the duke of Burgundy (shown here) created
the Order of the Golden Fleece, in memory of the Greek myth of
Jason. Members of orders swore to live up to the highest ideals.

The horse—a knight's best friend

The word "chivalry" comes from the French word *chevalier,* a knight. The word also means "horse-man," and without their horses knights would not have gotten very far. Horses were not just the only means of travel; they played an essential part in warfare. The strength of the cavalry charge could win or lose a battle.

In the Middle Ages horses were rather different from the ones you see today. They were swift and nervous, but they had to be strong enough to carry the weight of an armed man and a heavy harness through the commotion and jostling of battle. The warhorse was called a *destrier;* the word comes from the Latin *dextra,* meaning "right hand"; it is said that the horse was always led by the groom's right hand. For everyday use and for parades the lord rode a palfrey, which was lighter and more elegant.

Knights went to great lengths to obtain the finest horses, at first from England and Spain; then, once the crusades had started, Arab stallions became popular for their speed and alertness. Speed was all important in battle; horses had to be specially bred and trained to enable the knight to attack and attack again, wheeling around to launch yet another blow.

Until the 13th century knights carried only their arms on horseback while their baggage was carried on carts. But in the 14th century they began to wear very heavy armor, weighing 18 to 20 kilos. This made the rider less mobile and was more dangerous for the horse, so protective coverings of cloth and leather were added, padded at the neck and rump. Later, horses were given chainmail and plate-armor which encumbered their movements, leading to disasters such as that suffered by the French at Agincourt.

42

A knight says farewell to his lady and friends
before leaving for war. His squire holds his warhorse with his right hand.

...or covering long distances quickly, horses were essential. Ladies, ...owever, found it difficult to sit astride the narrow saddles with their ...ng, full dresses. In the 14th century special saddles began to be ...ade, enabling women to sit sidesaddle.

Carts and carriages were used for journeys, but the front axle, which makes it easy to turn corners, was not invented until the 13th century. Ladies were not expected to ride long distances on horseback; they were carried in litters—their husbands, too, sometimes!

...e lord would choose different breeds of horse to carry out particular ...nctions. Servants and men-at-arms rode on strong horses called ...unceys or ordinary horses called hackneys. Baggage was carried on

the backs of packhorses, sturdy, short-legged animals. The lord himself rode proudly on his *destrier,* or warhorse, and he would have a palfrey as a parade horse—here being led by its bridle.

...the 14th century the warhorse was a powerful animal, able to carry ...knight in armor at full gallop and to stand up to collision with ...other horse, equally heavy. In battles there were often more horses ...ounded than men, so many lords had armor made for them.

Horses needed a lot of looking after. *Destriers* were fed on oats two or three times a day and groomed night and morning, while the stables were kept impeccably clean. The castle had to keep enormous stores of fodder, and in a siege the horses always suffered.

An artist's view of a joust in 1470. This miniature was painted for Philip the Good, Duke of Burgundy.

Jousts and tournaments

Jousts and tournaments were grand social occasions and a great opportunity for knights to show off their skills. Tournaments, or tourneys, first started in France. They were mock battles between two groups of mounted knights who fought with maces and blunted swords, trying to knock each other to the ground. Despite strict rules, men were sometimes killed in tourneys.

Jousts, combats between two knights on horseback, were held before or after the tournament in enclosures called "lists." Crowds thronged to see the combatants and their ladies, who sat in special stands wearing their finest dresses. The herald called for silence and introduced the competitors, singing the praises of each one. Then the first two knights charged at each other, lances poised, each trying to break the other's lance or knock him from his horse.

The overall winner was given a prize by a lady who had been chosen as Queen of Beauty.

When a lord decided to hold a tournament he invited all his friends and vassals. The countryside buzzed with excitement as contestants and onlookers poured in from all around. The lord lodged his guests in the castle and when that overflowed he put up tents for them outside. Tournaments lasted several days, interspersed with banquets, singing, dancing, and entertainment by mummers.

Some knights made their fortunes going from tourney to tourney, like the Englishman William Marshal, hero of about 500 tournaments. Once, after he had dismounted 203 knights, his helmet was so battered by blows that a blacksmith had to help him get it off! He needed two clerks to add up his winnings.

he Middle Ages people enjoyed rough sports like wrestling, which
es back to ancient times. These sports were a good way of keeping
physical training when warfare was common, as in the 14th and
th centuries during the Hundred Years' War.

ights spent a lot of time in training exercises like riding at the
ntain. This was a wooden dummy fixed on a pivot and fitted with a
eld and a heavy beam. If the knight rode too slowly or aimed his
ce wrong, it would swing around and give him a painful blow.

e tournament was a mock battle between two groups of men.
metimes they were held to settle private quarrels, and then the
rnament could become a real battle. Men were often killed in the
citement of the *mêlée*—the hand-to-hand fighting.

A knight is about to enter the lists. His squire buckles his armor and a
servant stands by with his three-pronged lance. Competitors learned
to recognize each other by their coats of arms. Chivalry included
courtly behavior toward the ladies.

A victorious knight was given a prize of arms, armor, a horse, and
sometimes large sums of money by his unfortunate adversary. Some
knights became rich and famous through their exploits at tournaments; they were fighters to be reckoned with.

In the heat of battle

When an enemy appeared on the castle lands the lord and his men had a choice—to let themselves be besieged or to come out from behind their walls and do battle. In this picture the knights have taken up their arms and mounted their *destriers* to face the enemy outside.

During the course of the centuries armor underwent a great many changes. Originally knights were armed with a pike, a mace, a lance, a sword, and sometimes a battle-axe. To protect themselves they had helmets, round or oval shields, and long coats of mail. The famous Bayeux Tapestry shows many illustrations of soldiers fighting in coats of mail. They gave strong protection in the battles of those times.

However, when gunpowder began to be used around 1330, better protection was needed. Plates of steel were added on the chest, arms, legs, and feet, and the knight wore steel gauntlets. Helmets covered the head completely, not unlike crash helmets; their rounded shape made it easier to avoid blows. By the end of the 14th century the knight was completely encased in steel, like the ones shown here. Shields were no longer so necessary; they were smaller in size and served to deflect the blows of the enemy's lances.

The main action in a battle was the charge: the two sides launched themselves at each other and tried to knock each other down. Once thrown to the ground a rider was lost; imprisoned in his armor, he was at the mercy of his adversary, who could finish him off with a simple dagger thrust. But if possible the enemy preferred to capture the knight alive and demand a high ransom for him. On the battlefield the victor took what trophies he could, seizing the vanquished man's armor and his horse—or, if the horse was wounded, its harness.

46

The first engagement in a battle. The knights stand in their saddles, armed with lances and shields, and try to overthrow each other.

re the battle the herald visited the outskirts of the enemy
p, wearing his tabard with his lord's arms on it. He blew the
npet three times and loudly proclaimed the challenge. Heralds
e not armed; they held a position of immunity as messengers.

If a castle hadn't the means to stand up to a long siege, the garrison
would make a sortie through the barbican. They would leave the
entrance open to allow convoys of food to get in. Sometimes the
besiegers themselves suffered from starvation.

ghts in full charge—the most glorious and fearsome moment of
battle. Few combatants could withstand this wave of some
ns of horses bearing their steel-clad riders, and those who could
on their horses had reason to be proud of themselves. The

best way of defending a castle under enemy attack was to block
he entrances by encircling them with a series of stone walls and
den stockades. Villages, too, were defended in the same effec-
way.

outcome of the battle was often decided by the charge. However, in
the 14th century during the Hundred Years' War, it was the archers,
on foot, who were unbeatable. In battles like Crécy and Agincourt the
English archers inflicted terrible damage on the French cavalry.

At the end of a battle it was customary to bury the dead and remove
the wounded. Here the herald had a part to play, because he could
identify the corpses by their coats of arms. If the victor managed to
take a knight prisoner, he could demand a heavy ransom for him.

Crusades—the holy wars

Following the example of King Louis IX of France as well as many others since 1096, Sir de Joinville of Champagne, France, joined a crusade to the Holy Land. Filled with sadness at leaving his home and family, he left his castle humbly, on bare feet, and dressed in a simple woolen garment. He and his knights paused to pray at several shrines along their way, while their horses and equipment were taken directly to the port of Marseilles to await their arrival.

A month later they arrived at Marseilles, where the ships that would carry them to the Holy Land were waiting. The horses entered the hold through a special hatch, which was sealed against sea water.

"Set sail in the name of God!" cried the ship's captain. And so began the great adventure.

The first crusaders had traveled overland, taking ten months to reach Turkey, where they struck the first blows against the Infidel. After that many crusaders preferred the shorter sea route, embarking at Barcelona, Marseilles, Pisa, or Genoa, with stopovers at Bari and Malta. But this route was also dangerous. They might be attacked by the Muslim pirates who haunted the coasts of North Africa, cheated by Greek or Italian traders, or betrayed by the Emperor of Constantinople—all before arriving to face the fierce Muslim armies. Often the journey ended not in the planned pilgrimage to Jerusalem, but with death or, even worse, capture and slavery at the hands of the Infidels. But for 200 years from the end of the 11th century, crusading was a Christian duty for all knights, from the humblest baron to the proudest prince. (In some cases kings and princes got rid of troublesome vassals by packing them off on a crusade!)

Once they reached the Holy Land, the Christian princes organized a whole network of fortresses to protect the territory they had won from the Turks. They built castles to defend mountain passes and protect the access to harbors; and great forts, like Krak des Chevaliers, standing on rocky spurs where they could overlook hills and valleys. Castle-building was further advanced than in the West, and the masons took the new techniques back to Europe with them. Some crusaders settled down and made their homes in *Outremer* (overseas), the states they set up in the Holy Land.

The kings of England and France set off to defend the Holy Land. The round-bottomed ships are packed to overflowing.

king a vow to join a crusade was part of the knight's code of valry. Here a knight says farewell to his family; his wife is pecting a baby so she can't go with him as wives often do. The lord ll be away for a year or two.

get to the Holy Land, crusaders perferred to go by sea rather than erland, which took much longer. The prows and sterns of the little ps were raised high above the water and fortified like miniature tles; this explains the word "foc's'le," or "forecastle."

his way home from the crusades, Richard the Lionhearted was pwrecked and fell into the hands of an enemy. A huge ransom was nanded for his release, and his mother, Eleanor of Aquitaine, ected the money. All his vassals contributed to it.

In the Holy Land the crusaders defended their territory against the Muslim Turks—the Infidels. They built a large number of forts including the fortress of Soâne, shown here. To make it really strong they defended it with a ditch 28 meters deep and 20 meters wide.

Left alone in the castle, the lord's wife had to run the estate. Highborn women were trained in business and legal matters, and their orders were "cried" around the estate by heralds. If war broke out in the lord's absence, the garrison chief took his orders from the lady.

The birth of heraldry

Since soldiers didn't wear uniforms, combatants had to have some way of distinguishing each other in battle. One means of recognition was the rallying cry shouted by each side to summon the men to their lord and his banner. Another was for men on the same side to wear emblems on their armor. Gradually these developed into the "devices" or patterns which made up the complete "blazons" or coats of arms that were painted on shields. The shields, made of metal and wood, were covered in leather which was then painted in different colors, called "tinctures," and "metals," gold and silver, to form stripes, crosses, bands, and so on. In the 12th century these devices were added to, the most common symbols being crosses, lilies, the eagle, and the lion. Finally there were so many that registers had to be drawn up listing and illustrating all the known coats of arms. They were called "armorials" or "rolls of arms" (they were painted on long rolls of parchment).

Everyone knew the coats of arms of neighboring lords, but in times of war knights might come from far afield and their arms would not be known. So the lord employed a herald, whose job it was to know all of them. The art of identifying coats of arms thus became known as heraldry.

You could tell who the herald was by the fact that he went unarmed, with no lance or sword, and by his tabard, a sleeveless tunic embroidered with the arms of his lord. He was untouchable, almost sacred. Only he was allowed to enter the enemy camp to carry messages. Before they set forth into battle the knights entrusted him with their money or their wills, and during the fighting the heralds stood on one side, observing or running messages. Afterwards it was their job to count the dead and identify the bodies by their coats of arms.

In the 14th century the coats of arms of different lords became so varied and complex that experts, the heralds, drew up lists of them called armorials, illustrating each one.

In the early days of the Middle Ages battles were completely chaotic. Knights had no uniforms, so in order to tell who was on which side they painted their personal emblems on their shields. Later, the coat of arms was depicted within the shape of a shield.

Many coats of arms have their origins in tales of valor. We are told, for example, that during the Battle of Ptolemais, the Duke of Austria was completely covered in blood except for the area round his belt. The red and white colors of the Austrian flag commemorate the story.

There is a strict heraldic language to describe coats of arms, or escutcheons. They are made up of combinations of "tinctures" and "metals," in geometric designs (1–4); patterns based on fur like ermine (5) and "vair"—squirrel (6); and emblems like the cross (8),

A lord's arms were placed all around the castle—on the walls, at the top of pillars, and above the door. If the castle was captured, the new owner lost no time in removing the traces of his predecessor and replacing them with his own arms.

the fleur de lys (9), the lion (10), the eagle (11), and the leopard (12). They could be divided up into any number of "quarterings" (7). The colors are given special names: "or" (gold) = yellow, "argent" (silver) = white, "azure" = blue, "gules" = red, and "sable" = black.

There were other ways of distinguishing men in battle. The Scottish kilt, for example, was woven in stripes of different widths and colors crossing each other to form the "tartans" which belonged to different clans.

A walled town being defended against besiegers, 1460. The archers are using longbows and crossbows.

Under siege

Our picture shows an attack in full force. It's a hot day, and one man breaks off from fighting to quench his thirst. Along the town walls the defenders are using all their strength and wits to repulse the attackers. They feel fairly safe—from the tops of the walls they can bombard the assailants with stones, wood, melted lead, scalding liquids, even rubbish. They are able to do this where the walls are divided by crenellations and from towers with projecting machicolations. Plain walls are more difficult to defend. On the right they have had to position bundles of burning tow to keep the enemy off.

The attackers beneath the walls would have gained nothing by attacking immediately; they have waited some time for the defenders to become weakened by hunger, thirst, and fatigue. When the judge that the time to attack is ripe, the foot soldier start climbing the walls while the archers cover them and prevent the defenders from pushing their ladder away. The bowmen at the rear are using the cross bow, a more accurate and lethal weapon than th longbow—in fact in the 12th century the Churcl condemned its use. It was also a delicate and expensive instrument.

If all the usual methods fail, the attackers ma construct a wooden siege tower to enable them t climb over the walls. It will have to be protected wit wet skins, for the enemy will try to set it on fire. An when they have crossed the ramparts there are sti many obstacles for them to face!

...der the wooden roof at the top of a tower, a handful of men try to ...e off the enemy attack. They drop down on the enemy anything ... have available—scalding liquids, melted lead, pitch, stones— ...n furniture and rubbish if they've nothing else to throw.

...h an ordinary longbow you could shoot an arrow 90 cm long about ... meters. The crossbow was even more accurate, and it shot a ...al bolt with a four-sided head. The first firearms were not much ...e powerful, but the shot could go through armor.

...d being delivered to a besieged castle overlooking the sea. A boat ...reach the very foot of the walls and the besiegers can do nothing ...event it. Under these conditions a siege could last several weeks ...ven months.

The besiegers attempt an attack. Some of them are mining the base of the walls to make a breach. But the people in the castle are still fighting back from the walls and the "hourds," the long wooden protective galleries built along the tops of walls and towers.

Very few castles were actually taken by force. But if there was a traitor inside, the garrison was lost. He would secretly let enemy soldiers in to open the gate and let down the drawbridge. The defenders, taken by surprise, would have no choice but to surrender.

Early cannons being used to deal the final blow to a besieged castle.

The decline of the castle

A siege could go on a long time, and the people inside, hungry and often ill, would become increasingly demoralized. There were holes in the walls and towers, and shrubs and bushes had grown up on the castle mount, making it easier for the enemy to approach. When the attackers moved cannons onto the scene the siege would soon be at an end.

Gunpowder was first used in the early 14th century. The first cannons fired large arrows and created more noise than damage. They were less effective in siege warfare than the old siege engines like the trebuchet, which hurled heavy rocks. But artillery developed rapidly; by 1377 there were cannons that could fire a 90-kilogram ball. In the 15th century they became even more powerful and accurate, able to shoot fireballs into the very heart of a castle.

By the end of the 15th century the castle had lost its original role. Kings ruled over clearly defined kingdoms and had their armies, law officers, and justice officials to maintain order and peace. Towns were expanding and the rural population growing. Often the local lord preferred to build himself a new home in the style of the period—grand palaces, like Hampton Court Palace built for Henry VIII of England, and the elegant châteaux along the Loire Valley in France. So many castles were abandoned, or used for other purposes—as prisons, or for storage.

But castles did not die out completely; they went on being built into the 18th century, and used as refuges when necessary. Some were the scenes of fierce fighting during the two world wars.

hen a lord overcame a rebellious vassal or a troublesome neighbor, would often make it part of the peace terms that his castle should pulled down. He would send an official to see that the job was done operly.

Gradually firearms became really powerful. In the 15th century, although they could not yet demolish curtain walls or towers, they were capable of firing missiles through the wooden defenses. Once a gate was destroyed the attackers could pour in.

the years went by, castles, once so necessary for keeping the ace, became no more than grand homes for local lords. They no ger surveyed the countryside in solitary state. Houses, villages, d towns clustered around their walls.

high walls of castles were an easy and vulnerable target for nnon fire, so military architects began to build low-lying fortresses. e Château of Salses (shown here) lies between Languedoc in the th of France and Catalonia in Spain. Building began in 1497 and it

By the end of the 15th century lords were no longer so concerned about defending themselves. They wanted comfortable and elegant homes to live in. Some of them would meet architects on their travels and bring them home to design a new, lighter, sunnier palace.

was first besieged in 1503. Its design was revolutionary for the times, crouching behind a defense of earthworks in the center of a plain. In the 17th century the famous French architect Vauban regularly followed this plan, and modern forts are built along the same lines.

Great castles

Where to find them

Along the Rhine

The great rivers of Europe were vital routes for the expansion of trade, and also provided a good means of travel for foreign invaders—two good reasons for building castles.

All along the route of the Rhine valley stands a chain of fortresses, stretching from Switzerland to Belgium.

At Kaub there are two castles, each an example of a different period. Above is the castle of Gutenfels (meaning "Good Cliff"), whose chief feature is the Berg-fried (Belfrey) Tower. This type of tower stands alone with no moat or motte. It overlooks the surrounding area, commanding a view of rivers and lakes, which is why the Germans refer to it as a *Wasserturm,* a "water tower." In the 14th century this type of defense was no longer enough, and Louis III, Emperor of Bavaria, abandoned the upper castle to build a new fortress on an island. This castle, the Pfalzgrafenstein, was built along the lines of a ship, and seems to be sailing along in mid-river. It was used as a toll station; passing boats had to pay a fee as they went by.

THONIG — ZEFA

Two German castles: Gutenfels on the hill and the Pfalzgrafenstein on the Rhine.

# of Europe

Eltz, in Germany

The Muiderslot, a brick castle

In Holland there is not much good building stone to be found naturally. There are few Dutch castles dating from before the 13th century, but from then on they began to be built in brick.

With the development of artillery it became clear that brick stood up well to cannon and gunfire; it was more resilient to the onslaught of missiles, and brick walls hold together better than stone ones. The castle at Muiden in Holland, called the Muiderslot, was built on the site of a 10th-century wooden tollhouse. It was a direct imitation of French and English castles, with a square bailey flanked at the corners by four round towers. But there are no machicolations along the walls; the castle was well enough defended from attack by the river which encircles it. The entrance gate, however, is heavily fortified.

The Muiderslot, in the Netherlands

The home comforts of Eltz

Many German castles are quite different inside from the impression they give outside.

When visitors first arrive they are confronted by typical fortresses with defenses of high walls, towers, and a barbican. But inside they are like tiny medieval towns. The outer walls of the living quarters are decorated with half-timbering; there are plenty of windows to light the rooms; and the courtyards are overhung by roofed galleries called loggias.

At Eltz there is a picturesque arrangement with four sets of living quarters facing into the courtyard. This came about in the 16th century when four members of the Eltz family inherited the castle. Each refused to surrender his share, so it was divided up among them.

Eltz is much more of a home than a fortress. It has all the conveniences that were modern in the 14th century—plumbing, toilets, and heating—and all the living rooms are decorated with magnificent wall paintings.

Ghent, a thousand years of building

The counts of Flanders began to be powerful figures in the 11th century. They were among the leaders of the First Crusade, and Flemish knights were the first to besiege Jerusalem.

When he returned from the crusade, the count of Flanders, Philip of Alsace, found that the citizens of Ghent had been trying to gain too much independence. To keep them down and to demonstrate his superior strength, he restored an old fortress dating from the Viking invasion. In 1180 he reinforced the keep and built a curtain wall around it, set with hanging turrets. In the 14th century this castle, called the Gravensteen, lost its military appearance and was turned into a real palace. All the stages of its building can still be seen.

The Gravensteen, in Belgium

57

Karlštejn, a giant jewel box

On June 10, 1348, the archbishop of Prague laid the foundation stone of this building in the presence of Charles IV, King of Bohemia.

King Charles intended the castle less as a military fortress than as a private residence which would also symbolize his power and authority. The keep, 37 meters high, is an impressive sight. Its main purpose was to house the crown jewels and relics of the saints. The king got the idea for this building in France, where he grew up, but he wanted its role to be purely symbolic. In fact Karlštejn was beseiged only once, in the 15th century during the Hussite Wars between Protestants and Catholics.

King Charles himself was a far from ordinary character. Although he continued to govern his country, he would spend weeks at a time alone in his castle chapel, living the life of a monk. His only means of communication with the outside world was a hole through which people handed him his food and the most urgent documents.

To make sure of an heir, Charles IV married four times. One of his wives was afraid that he might be attracted to the young court beauties, so she prepared a love potion and gave it to him—luckily for her, it didn't poison him!

His last wife was an unusually strong woman. The king amused himself by getting her to chop wood and tear up parchments in front of the Court.

Karlštejn, in Czechoslovakia

SITENSKY — ZEFA

Chillon, gateway to the Alps

Passes through mountains were few and far between, so traders had to follow certain fixed routes. This gave the castle owners along the way an opportunity to demand tolls from them.

The Château of Chillon was originally built to control the shipping on Lake Geneva. In the 11th century the bishops of Sion built the tower and an outer line of fortifications. In the 13th century the count of Savoy, then master

Chillon, in Switzerland

OF. NAT. SUISSE TOUR

of Chillon, decided to make the most of its naturally strong site on a rocky island. His architect drew up a compact design, with perfect defenses on the side facing the shore. On the lake side there was no need for fortifications, for no attacker would approach from that side. There was no shortage of fresh water, should a siege occur. The only drawback was the need to build enormous vaults for storage—later used as dungeons. The castle remained unchanged until 1536, when it was captured by the people of Berne, then a mighty city-state. Their bailiff decided to make it his residence, and the interior was converted to make it more comfortable.

Today visitors can still see the wall paintings and some of the hangings that decorated the living quarters. Like many castles that are still standing, Chillon has been restored several times, but it remains almost unchanged in appearance.

EVERTS — RAPHO

Peñafiel, in Spain

Peñafiel, a ship on a hill

This Spanish castle overlooks the valley of Douro in the province of Valladolid. The name Peñafiel means "faithful rock." A first castle was built on the site in the 11th century after the region had been recaptured from the Arabs by Sancho Garcia.

In the 15th century the military Order of Calatrava decided to fortify the hillside by building on it an absolutely impregnable fortress. The architects decided on a simple plan in the style called "gran buque," which means "great ship." At the center of this stone battleship rises a huge keep 34 meters high, fortified by hanging turrets. There is no direct way in; instead there are three staggered entrances.

Peñafiel symbolized the reconquest of Spain from the Arabs, whose power had already substantially diminished.

Pierrefonds, a fairy-tale castle

The duke of Valois began building the château of Pierrefonds in 1390. It is one of the best known examples of French military architecture, and was intended as a center of operations for the French to recapture northern France from the English. As it turned out, the theater of war moved some distance from the region and the castle, unused until 1588, was inherited by the kings of France.

In 1588 France was in the middle of its religious wars, and Pierrefonds was occupied by a ringleader who took advantage of the troubled state of affairs to ravage the countryside around. It took three successive sieges and a great deal of cannonfire to capture the castle from him. In 1616 the enemies of Louis XIII took refuge there, and it took 18,000 men six days to get them out!

Cardinal Richelieu, the king's chief minister, decided to prevent such incidents happening again by pulling the castle down and for 200 years Pierrefonds was nothing but a magnificent ruin.

Then, in 1857, Napoleon III decided to turn it into an imperial residence and asked the famous architect Viollet-le-Duc to restore it. The castle came to life again, though it was considerably changed along 19th-century lines. And that is the state it can be seen in today.

Pierrefonds, in France

Coucy, destroyed by 28 tons of explosives

Coucy was once a colossal castle, its entrance defended by a round tower 54 meters high and 31 meters across, surrounded by three curtain walls. The outer one completely enclosed the little town of Coucy.

Nowadays, little remains of the original castle. It was first ordered to be demolished in 1652, but the explosives used scarcely managed to crack the walls. Forty years later, an earthquake widened the cracks. Some restoration work was done in the 19th century, but in 1917 the German army blew up the keep—they had to use 28 tons of explosives to do it!

This giant once symbolized the power of a local family, the lords of Coucy. They had many adventures during the

Château of Coucy, in France

Middle Ages. One of them, Enguerrand VII, fought in Italy, Scotland, and Africa and was a candidate for the crown of Austria, but refused the position of Constable of France. The Coucy family did not belong to the ranks of the top French nobility, and they seem to have been proud of the fact. Their motto was:
"I am not king,
  Nor prince, nor duke, nor yet count.
  I am the Lord of Coucy."

Castel Coca, in Spain

The keep of the château of Coucy

Coca, a bishop's palace

Until the 12th century, castle building in Spain was hindered by the presence of the Arabs in that area. (You probably know the saying about "building castles in Spain," meaning "starting something that'll never get finished.") But by the end of the Middle Ages there were many fine castles all over the country.

The castle of Coca was built by the archbishop of Seville, a supporter of Queen Isabel of Castile. The work of building the castle was done by *mudejares,* Muslim workmen who had stayed on in the Christian part of Spain after it had been recaptured by the Catholics.

Most of the walls are built of bricks and decorated with curious patterns—stripes, chevrons, and herringbones, some painted and some made by using colored bricks. It was built on strongly military lines, fortified with turrets, towers, and machicolations. This fortress-like palace has only one entrance, defended by a tower. It was once a vital strategic point for Castile.

ROGER — VIOLLET

Alleuze, in France

Bonaguil, the pointless fortress

This superb castle was the result of one man's wounded pride. In 1482 Bérenger de Roquefeuil, Lord of Bonaguil, was summoned to appear before the Parliament of Toulouse, accused by one of his tenants of having withdrawn a particular privilege. The Parliament made a judgment against Bérenger.

Deeply mortified, the lord of Bonaguil retired to his estates, where stood a castle he had inherited from his father. He threw his entire fortune and all his energies into building a fortress the like of which had never been seen before. He doubled the curtain wall, had a huge moat dug and put up a drawbridge defended by a barbican.

After that he built a new curtain wall around it, lower than the rest, so that he could fire cannons over it. Bonaguil was fortified against all comers. Only—nobody ever went there! The only thing the castle had to protect was its owner's pride.

Right to the end of his life Bérenger went on obstinately putting everything he had into the creation of a perfect stronghold. And at the time of his death a totally different type of castle was being built—the elegant châteaux of Chinon and Chenonceaux.

Alleuze, a robber hideaway

Today Alleuze is a lonely ruin standing in the hills of the Auvergne region of France. But in the 14th century this ancient castle, owned by the bishops of Clermont, fell into the hands of a band of brigands, half English and half French. Their captain, Bernard de Garlans, made his living by kidnapping travelers and local peasants and demanding ransoms for them. And no one, it seemed, could force him out of his lair.

At last the king and the bishop proposed to the bandit leader that they should buy the castle back, this appearing to be the only way to get him out of it.

De Garlans dragged out the negotiations for several months, but finally the brigands left.

ARCHIVES PHOTOGRAPHIQUES

Bonaguil, in France

ROGER — VIOLLET

Château Gaillard, in France

Château Gaillard— the "Gallant Castle" laid low

This castle was built in a single year (1196–97) by Richard the Lionhearted, to defend the English possessions in Normandy. He was very proud of it and called it his "Gallant Castle"—Château Gaillard.

In 1203 it was besieged by his enemy King Philip Augustus of France. He started by occupying the surrounding region, forcing the local people (over a thousand of them) to take refuge in the castle. After two months the food ran low and the castle constable, Roger de Lacy, threw the people out to starve outside the walls.

Philip Augustus then had the moat filled in and set miners to work digging tunnels to undermine the towers. The French captured the outer bailey and the defenders retreated farther in. Suddenly, one night, the French managed to reach the heart of the castle by climbing through a drain hole in the wall. They lowered the drawbridge to let in their comrades and the garrison, taken completely by surprise, was forced to surrender.

In the 17th century Henry IV of France finished off its demolition.

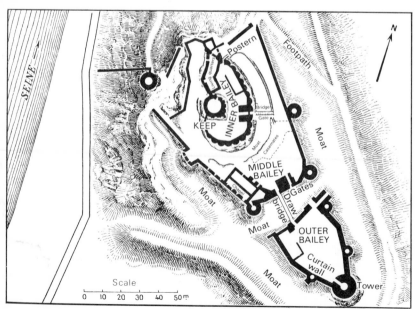

Plan of Château Gaillard

S. CAROUL

Castel del Monte, in Italy

Castel del Monte, built for the "Wonder of the World"

This beautiful castle is built of golden limestone and designed as a perfect octagon. There are octagonal towers at each corner, and the main rooms are trapezoids in shape to fit into this design.

Castel del Monte was built not as a military fortress but as a hunting lodge for the Holy Roman Emperor Frederick II of Hohenstaufen, who was nicknamed "Wonder of the World." He had a brilliant and luxurious court filled with poets and artists from East and West, and he built numerous castles to keep his name and reputation alive. In Castel del Monte he wanted to embody in a single building all the architectural knowledge of contemporary and classical times. Its building was started in 1240. It was decorated with statues and rich tapestries and carpets, and it had unusually advanced plumbing for the times.

Sirmione, a family stronghold

The castle of Sirmione lies on the banks of Lake Garda in northern Italy. It was built to supervise the water traffic and trading activities on the lake, and to collect tolls from the shipping.

Sirmione was the creation of a powerful Italian family, the Scaligeri, who ruled over the province of Verona in the 14th century. Throughout the Middle Ages the north of Italy was divided into two factions, one side supporting the emperor of the Holy Roman Empire and the other contesting his power. You can tell which lords were on which side by the style in which their castles were built. When the merlons, the section of parapet between two crenellations, have notches in them (as shown here), this indicates that the owner was on the emperor's side.

At the center of the castle rises a high tower, typical of the style of tower to be

Rochester, a castle defeated by roast pork

Most of the building of this castle was done in the 12th century, and the keep was completed in 1139. Rochester was strongly defended with curtain walls around the huge square keep. The towers were also square, and the keep was divided down the center by a wall something like the watertight bulkhead of a ship.

The castle was built of small-sized stones and originally whitewashed. When it was attacked by King John's troops in 1215, the besiegers mined a tunnel leading to the base of one of the corner towers. They propped up the

J. VALENTINE

Rochester Castle, England

tunnel roof with heavy wooden beams, and piled into the space forty nice fat pig carcasses. Then they set fire to them. In the intense heat given off by the burning fat the masonry cracked and the corner of the tower began to crumble. The besiegers easily entered the keep and forced the defenders to surrender. Afterwards one chronicler wrote: "Men no longer put their trust in castles." But the fallen tower was later replaced.

ENIT

Sirmione, in Italy

found all over Italy. In some cities there are dozens of them. The Italian nobility lived in cities and conducted their private wars within the city walls. Allied families built their towers close to each other and linked them with bridges or underground passages. Sometimes, when two opposing factions met, the streets and marketplaces ran with blood. This was the background of the famous story of Romeo and Juliet.

Dover Castle, in England

Dover Castle, a Plantagenet masterpiece

Henry Plantagenet, Count of Anjou, became king of England in 1154. He already owned the Loire region and Aquitaine in France, through his marriage to Eleanor of Aquitaine, so his new kingdom was divided by the English Channel.

To protect the sea route linking Anjou to England, Henry decided to build a strong fortress on the coast at Dover. The ruins of an ancient Roman lighthouse already stood on the site, and some fortifications had also been built there prior to the invasion by William the Conqueror.

Dover Castle has three lines of defense: an outer curtain wall (pulled down in the 18th century to make room for cannons); a second curtain wall, still standing; and in the middle a keep flanked by four square towers. This was the biggest keep to be built in the 12th century. Its walls were enormously thick, so thick, in fact, that the architect was able to build small rooms in them. The wall of the keep is reinforced by a "batter": the base is widened to deflect enemy missiles and to make it impossible to undermine.

Dover was a kind of key to England. In 1216 it withstood assault by the French and thus prevented England from being invaded.

Beaumaris, the unfinished castle

At the end of the 13th century Edward I of England set about subduing the rebellious Welsh. To enforce his power he built a chain of massive fortresses in North Wales—all magnificent examples of medieval architecture. His architect was a Frenchman from Savoy, James of St George, who put into practice all the skills that westerners had learned from the Muslims during the crusades.

Beaumaris, the last of these castles, is "concentric": that is, the inner bailey is guarded by high walls and towers and surrounded by an outer bailey with a lower wall and small towers. It has no keep. It lies on flat land close to the sea, whose water was used to fill the moat. Many of the Welsh castles had equally strong sites beside the sea. At the top of the walls runs a wall gallery as well as a wallwalk, to enable the defenders to move quickly to any part of the castle.

In the summer of 1295 thousands of workmen were being employed to build Beaumaris, at vast expense. But in 1296 Edward ran into financial difficulties; though building continued for some time, the castle was never finished.

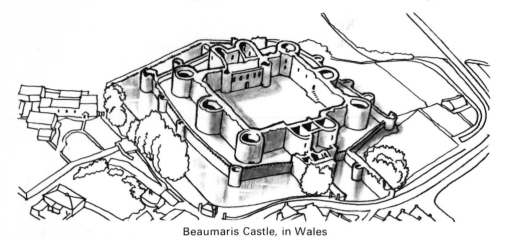

Beaumaris Castle, in Wales

Borthwick, a tower-house

Hundreds of medieval castles were built in Scotland, many of them still standing; legends are told of the ghosts that haunt them.

Few Scottish lords could afford to build great fortresses, but during the 14th and 15th centuries a large number of smaller "peels" or "tower-houses" were built, which served their purpose.

Borthwick Castle, one of these, was built in the 1430s by Sir William Borthwick, and the Borthwick family has lived there ever since. The architect deliberately gave it a grim, foreboding appearance. The building consists of a "two-slab" tower, a massive keep giving the appearance of two towers, rising starkly up and overshadowing the entrance gate. There are only a few small windows in these walls and no turrets to relieve their severity, though the tops of the towers are machicolated. Inside, there is a confusion of many staircases and passages.

A. BRITANNIQUE

Borthwick Castle, in Scotland

The revival of interest in castles

For almost three centuries castles underwent a period of neglect. In Europe they were pulled down on the orders of kings like Louis XIV of France, who wanted total power over their kingdoms. In England a large number of them played a role in the civil wars of the 17th century, and many were demolished by Cromwell. Many were simply abandoned by owners who preferred comfortable palaces and stately homes to live in. Their stones were used as building material, and their crumbling remains became the subject of legends and terrifying ghost stories.

At the end of the 18th century and the beginning of the 19th, artists and writers began to rediscover their charms. In England in the 1760s Horace Walpole wrote *The Castle of Otranto*, a novel based on a dream about a medieval castle, which remained extremely popular for years. Later the poets, painters, and composers of the Romantic Movement brought castles into their work. They were used as a background in paintings, and played a part in novels of adventure like those written by Sir Walter Scott.

In the mid-19th century a fashion developed for medieval romance and chivalry. Various people throughout Europe decided that some of the ancient castles should be restored, either for historical reasons or so that they could be turned into splendid homes. The architects of those days were not too concerned about historical accuracy: they put in iron girders, added Gothic-style decorations and installed central heating. Many wealthy people built entirely new "medieval" castles. One of the most famous of these people was Ludwig II, the mad king of Bavaria. Nevertheless, some good work was done and in France, for example, a number of castles like Pierrefonds owe their survival to the architect Viollet-le-Duc.

Today, archaeologists and historians who specialize in the Middle Ages are much more interested in historical accuracy. Their task is not always an easy one. How, for example, do you preserve a tower when its foundations are crumbling? How do you uncover 13th-century wall paintings without destroying the paintings which have been laid over them in later centuries? Sometimes the ruins are lying in the path of a proposed motorway or industrial development. These, and many others, are the kinds of problems the experts are trying to solve.

Nevertheless, the work of excavating and restoring these ancient buildings is being done with the greatest care and regard for detail. Groups of young people take part in the work as well.

The miniatures reproduced in this book were collected by Jean Vigne. Sources: p.34, Bibliothèque Nationale, Paris; pp. 12, 14, 20, 22, 24, 30, 40, 42, 44, 46, 48, 52, Arsenal Library, Paris; pp. 16, 28, 36, Municipal Library, Lyons; p. 42, Municipal Library, St. Dié; p. 26, Musée Condé, Chantilly. The drawings on pages 4, 5, and 59 are from *Album Historique—Le Moyen Age* by E. Lavisse, A. Colin, Paris, 1905. The illustrator and editor wish to thank Pierre Brochard for his help and efficiency. Coloring by Catherine Legrand. The 15th-century banquet scene on the cover is from the Dutuit Collection in the Petit Palais, Paris. Photograph by Hachette.

Glossary

Accolade A ceremony to make a man a knight; a tap on the shoulder with the flat of a sword

Armor A protective covering for the body

Armorial A book of coats of arms and their owners

Bailey The courtyard around a castle

Barbican A defense tower over a bridge or gate

Black Death Bubonic plague which killed many thousands of people in Europe in the 1300's.

Book of Hours A small prayer book of the Middle Ages; many were beautifully illustrated.

Casemate A strongly built chamber within the castle walls from which cannons could be fired

Castle A building constructed to withstand attacks, with towers and thick walls

Chivalry The unwritten customs and rules of knights of the Middle Ages

Coat of arms An identifying design worn on the shield or over the armor of a knight

Crenellations Open spaces along the top of the castle walls

Crusade A war by medieval kings and knights to regain the Holy Land for Christianity

Curtain wall The outer wall around a castle

Donjon A round tower, the most strongly fortified part of a castle

Drawbridge A movable bridge across a moat

Feudal system The social and economic system of western Europe in the Middle Ages

Fief Land given to a vassal to use in return for military and other services to a lord

Garrison The group of soldiers kept on hand to defend a castle

Hauberk A long coat or tunic of mail

Herald The man who carried messages in battle, identified combatants by their coats of arms, and announced contestants at tournaments

Heraldry The study and use of coats of arms

Holy Land Palestine; where the Crusades were fought

Homage The paying of respect by a vassal to his lord

Hourd A covered walkway around the top of the castle walls and towers

Infidel Holders of the Holy Land during the Crusades

Journeyman A skilled craftsman hired and paid by the day (from the French word *journée*, a day)

Joust A mock battle between two knights with lances on horseback

Keep The strongest part of a castle; the donjon

Knight A military servant of a lord; often raised to a special rank and committed to chivalrous behavior

List An enclosure for tournaments and jousting

Machicolation An opening in the floor of an overhanging wall or tower

Mail Armor made of links of chain or overlapping metal plates

Master mason The architect in charge of building a castle

Medieval Belonging to the Middle Ages

Merlon The solid part between two crenellations in the upper castle wall

Middle Ages The years between A.D. 400 and 1450

Minstrel A musician or singer who entertained the lords and ladies of the castle

Moat A deep, steep-sided ditch around a castle, often filled with water

Motte An earthen mound which held a tower and was surrounded by a wall and ditch

Noble A person of high rank, often lord of a castle and a landowner

Peasant A farmer in the working class

Portcullis Strong iron grating that could be lowered to block the entrance to a town or castle

Postern A back door or gate of a castle

Quintain A dummy used for practicing jousting

Quoits A game like horseshoes, played with iron rings

Seal A design stamped on wax, used by a lord or lady instead of a signature. Also, the stamp used to make the design

Serf A slave who belonged to the land he worked on and was bought and sold with the land

Siege The act of surrounding a castle or town to cut off supplies and to attack the walls

Tapestry A cloth with a woven design or picture

Tournament A competition between groups of knights, conducted according to certain rules

Tower-house A small fortified tower; the cattle lived on the ground level, and the living quarters above were reached by movable stairs

Troubadour A wandering poet or composer

Turret A small tower

Vassal A person who owes homage and services to a king or noble in exchange for land

Index

2 3 4 5 6 7 8 9 10—11–85 84